THE FLU SEASON

BY WILL ENO

★

★

DRAMATISTS
PLAY SERVICE
INC.

THE FLU SEASON was originally produced by the Gate Theatre in London in April 2003, directed by Erica Whyman. The first U.S. production was by the Rude Mechanicals Theater Company at the Blue Heron Arts Center in New York City, opening on January 29, 2004. It was directed by Hal Brooks; the set design was by David Korins; the costume design was by Becky Lasky; the lighting design was by Mark Barton; the sound design was by Sloan Alexander; and the original music and music supervision were by Mike Errico. The cast was as follows:

PROLOGUE	Matthew Lawler
EPILOGUE	David Fitzgerald
MAN	Andrew Benator
WOMAN	Roxanna Hope
NURSE	Elizabeth Sherman
DOCTOR	Scott Bowman
TELEVISION	James Urbaniak

DRAMATIS PERSONAE

PROLOGUE, a narrator. Male. He should differ — if not physically, at least in terms of demeanor — from Epilogue. In physical terms, perhaps Prologue is large, and Epilogue is skinny. More importantly, where Prologue should tend toward warmth and geniality in his demeanor, Epilogue should seem colder, more angular, should maybe even have a flair for a seductive kind of cruelty. That said, they are both narrators, after all, and are therefore generally restrained in their manner; so that whatever feelings they have about the play and its story (and they should have many strong feelings) should be seen more in their suppression than in their expression. We should see them managing (with a couple of exceptions, mainly in Prologue's case) to overcome the force of their feelings, or, to deny those feelings, or avoid them altogether. Though none of this should be played too obviously. The general effect, and this is true of most of the characters in *The Flu Season*, should be similar to watching a pane of glass slowly break (to use a metaphor). These are very particular notes describing a very particular effect; don't let them be confusing. There is nothing here that is not in Hamlet's speech to the players (Act III, sc. 2). Play it simply and straightforwardly, with all the dignity, comedy, and tragedy that naturally occurs in the human animal. Prologue and Epilogue believe what they are saying, they care about the audience (though in very different ways). The play has a close relation to each of their identities and histories, so the stakes are always high for each of them. Both narrators remain onstage, except where noted. Finally, though Prologue is not aware of Epilogue, the latter is aware of the former.

EPILOGUE, a narrator. Male. As described above.

MAN, late twenties.

WOMAN, late twenties.

DOCTOR, male, fifties, doctoral, dignified though somewhat distracted.

NURSE, female, early fifties, maternal, also dignified though somewhat distracted.

SETTING

The play takes place in a mental health institution of a not very specific type. (Though not specific, it is very certainly not meant to be any kind of shocking or cruel environment. *The Flu Season* is not a criticism of the mental health industry. It is a play about the difficulty of love, the difficulty of being human, of making art.) The play also takes place in a theatre, as each narrator makes clear.

The Flu Season could be called an experimental play. It uses some complicated strategies. It should not be played or staged as a complicated or radically experimental play. All elements should simply be used to tell the story, the whole story, as powerfully and plainly as possible. Proceeding this way should produce an effect which is brave and new and moving, rather than just "experimental" for the sake of being experimental.

ACTS AND SCENES

There are two acts. The first is made up of nine scenes. The second, twelve scenes.

GENERAL NOTES ABOUT PEOPLE AND ACTING

People are complicated and behave in ironic and self-contradicting ways that can be seen as tragic or comic, and, often, as both, simultaneously. We can contradict ourselves, often severely, almost effortlessly. And we live with near-constant anxiety, though almost all of it is buried beneath our normal behavior. The same is true for the characters in this play. This does not mean that the complication and irony or anxiety of the characters needs to be "played" in any blatant way. On the contrary. The strongest performance, the most human and most forceful, will often be the simplest. Though the language in the play is not necessarily naturalistic, it is, on the other hand, how these characters naturally speak. This is how it comes out of them. Attention should be paid, in rehearsal, to finding a delivery or a way of performance that, on the one hand, serves the heightened nature of the language and the heightened nature of the characters' circumstances; and, on the other hand, serves to create real and believable characters who speak real and believable lines. They should be comfortable, for the most part, with the words they speak (though they may be uncomfortable with the situations in which they speak them). See, again, Hamlet's speech in Act III, Scene 2. Running times will vary, but, in general, pauses should be avoided, except where called for.

Finally, and importantly, it is the author's very strong feeling and belief that: PROLOGUE and EPILOGUE are narrators, yes. But, it might also be that they (particularly EPILOGUE) have, in an earlier life, suffered the fate of WOMAN. Or suffered the fate of some of the other characters in the play. Thus, their relation to the play is real and immediate and based in feeling; MAN and WOMAN are not "crazy people," but are simply people trying to live in the world in which they find themselves; DOCTOR and NURSE are not unkind, are not even necessarily ineffective, but instead are simply people who are trying to help, despite being somewhat distracted by their own private pains. If the play is played simply and seriously, the effect can be quite profound, quite funny and sad.

GENERAL NOTES ABOUT STAGING

Sets should be simple. Sets should also allow for quick transitions between scenes (In fact, the play can move along almost seamlessly, with transitions being made while narrators narrate. Though, if done this way, it should be done sensitively and with meaning, and not just for the sake of speed.). *The Flu Season* is very much a play, as each narrator often reminds us; so, directors and producers should not put too much money or energy into lavish sets in an effort to make believable what can most be made believable by the actors' performances. Also, a certain humility about theatre is expressed by the play, and, this humility might be undone by particularly ornate or complicated scenery.

"We tell our little story, staring out. We devise the beginning knowing the end, and this is trouble. We trudge on, into the winter, losing ground, looking back, trying, telling a tale of summer, a sinking feeling amid the leaving geese and slush. It's coming, little one. Truth. Real cold. Now, where's my shoes?"

—*from the film* By Dint of the Bridge's Collapse

THE FLU SEASON

ACT ONE

Scene 1

PROLOGUE. *(Enters, in darkness. Footsteps. Pause.)* Darkness and footsteps. A little pause. *(Pause.)* It's quiet and dark. But you knew that. *(Pause.)* I could leave it all alone, let us shudder by ourselves, leave us uncomforted by the shaky fiction of anything shared, of any common story. I could let us wreck ourselves in the dark, shiver closer to death, slowly, unnoticeably, instead of making such a big production out of it. But I won't. So, savor it, the dark. Like everything, it's ending. Yes, as for the darkness, at least: The End. *(Lights up.)* Hello. My name is Prologue. Welcome to a play whose title is *The Snow Romance.* It is a chronicle of love and no love, of interiors and exteriors, of weather, change, entry-level psychology, and time; but, oh, lo — what chronicle isn't. Composed one spring, it follows the lives of four or five people living in the season just previous. I'll be brief. We are in a sort of hospital. The time is almost winter. The lights fall. *(The lights don't fall.)*

EPILOGUE. Right. *(A brief pause.)* A couple quick things. About the title, the play is now called *The Flu Season.* A lot of downtime has gone by since the first draft was written, or, quote, composed. The new title stands for the fatigue, for all the sick-days, the sick years, wasted in coming up with a title at all. *The Flu Season.* I don't know. Could use some work, another year of scribbling, erasing. There's always a different word, some other title, something better the language might cough up. My character, we'll call him *Epilogue.* Could have also been called *Regrets.* Or, *Mr. Sorry-So-Sorry.* Could have been called, I don't know, *Steve Stevenson,* the names don't matter. Can you hear me okay? Can you see me? *(Motioning to Prologue.)* He can't. Strange. Theatre. This. Certain things we have to live with. Little rules and lies. Anyway, I come later, after; a little more — maybe — coldly. I'll revise a line, add an afterthought, subtract a feeling. I'll try to speak plainly. But I liked that last part. It describes life. I quote: "I'll be brief. We are in a sort of hospital. The time is almost winter. The lights fall." *(Lights down on Prologue and Epilogue. Man is sitting downstage, left or right, in very low light. The Woman and Nurse scene will take place on the other side of the stage, and they can be seated there, now, in darkness, while Man and Doctor scene is played.)*

DOCTOR. *(Enters upstage.)* All alone in the all-dark, are we? Sitting in the twilight of the exit light, licking our wounds with our wounded tongue, dreaming of some great difference, some healing hand, some heavenly or electrical light? Or just sitting there? Which? There is a difference. Tell us. The shuffling coughing world awaits. Give us a little of your disquiet.

MAN. I'm not doing anything.

DOCTOR. Well, not anything or not, we still need the light. *(He turns on a light switch. Lights up.)* It adds a sort of decorum to our proceedings, brightens up the otherwise muted décor of our shadowy procession. And it helps us see. But how was it, without it?

MAN. Darker.

DOCTOR. I see. Less light. But what about you? How are you?

MAN. No.

DOCTOR. *(Pause.)* I'm sorry? I said, "How are you?"

MAN. I'm sorry, I thought you said, "Who are you?"

DOCTOR. *(Brief pause.)* Even if I had, wouldn't "No" still have been the wrong answer?

MAN. The mind doesn't work this way.

DOCTOR. What way?

MAN. Responsively. I don't know. Responsively.

DOCTOR. I'm sorry?

MAN. Nothing. Can I go lie down?

DOCTOR. First, I have to quickly ask you a question or two.

MAN. *(He takes a very large breath in and holds his breath. He speaks with great difficulty.)* Yur tha dogdor. You know bess.

DOCTOR. The first question is, *(He reads.)* "In your personal dealings with people, with the certain persons who people your immediate surroundings, have you ever personally felt it humanly necessary to present, solely for the sole and lone purpose of individuality itself, a persona, such that ... " *(Man, still holding breath, is turning blue. Doctor sees this.)* This is not that important. Would you like to go lie down?

MAN. *(Huge exhalation.)* I really would.

DOCTOR. We can talk later. I do need you to sign something. Nothing very serious or breathtaking, just more paper for the future to shred. A form. Strictly a formality. *(Doctor begins to fill out a form.)*

MAN. *(Man is watching Doctor from across the desk.)* How do you do that?

DOCTOR. Do what?

MAN. Write upside-down like that?

DOCTOR. *(Doctor flips the paper around, showing that he was writing right-side up.)* Voila!

MAN. Oh, right. I get so used to seeing things from my own perspective.

DOCTOR. I see. From *my* own, I guess, yes? Please sign.

MAN. *(He signs.)* Voila. *(Looking at his signature.)* Look at that. It really is strictly a formality. This is me — strictly, formally me — but it's not the only me. There's a hundred ways I could do it, all different, all mine. Looking at my little slanted mess of a signature, I have to wonder where my life will take me.

DOCTOR. I'll show you your room.

MAN. *(Looking back down at signature.)* I should have seen that somehow. *(Doctor and Man exit. Nurse and Woman are on the other side of the stage. Nurse at desk, Woman seated before it. Lights up.)*

NURSE. I think that would be fine.

WOMAN. *(Pause.)* What would? No one said anything. You're just going to start talking to me, totally out of the blue?

NURSE. I am. I think people will understand. Maybe you've seen a baby born, or a grown-up die. Amazing. Totally out of the blue. And, as someone once said to someone, everything has to start somewhere.

WOMAN. Well, so, then, start.

NURSE. In fact, dear, we're almost finished. So, lastly, any allergy or injury or personal personal history that you would like to make public. Any distinguishing marks, inside or out? A birthmark in the shape of anything? Some internalized agony wholly without form? Any even sketchy sense of your character to help us empathize with you, to help us live more empathically, more heroically, within the life-size form of our own familiar pain?

WOMAN. No.

NURSE. Splendid. I will duly note that. *(She writes for fifteen seconds in her notebook.)*

WOMAN. Are they still spelling "No" with just two letters, or is it more, now?

NURSE. Oh, this — I'm sorry. I'm just scribbling. You're probably wondering where my little scribbles will take you. Yes? Either way, it all comes to something. A period, at least. A comma, or, dot-dot-dot, in some sad cases. *(Pause.)* Well, I think you'll be a wonderful —

WOMAN. *(Interrupting.)* No, I won't. I won't be a wonderful anything. Whatever noun was about to come out of you. I'll be here until I leave here, and I was only here because some family — reportedly mine — brought me here, and left me here.

NURSE. Families are only groups of people. And groups of people mean well, they try. Unless they're angry mobs waving broken bottles and golf clubs, and even then, they still — in their way — try. Here we also try to create a familial atmosphere. Or at least we try to act like a group of people. And the grounds are beautiful, this lovely time of year. The temperature dropping. Fall. Us, trying. The wonderful maple trees.

WOMAN. Yes, wonderful wonderful. Beautiful trees shedding their leaves, as I disintegrate into an animal, snow gently falling onto the uncombed hair of me, a cold cold girl, a sometime bitch in heat.

NURSE. Yes, well, you're tired, I'm sure, and possibly a little more elegiac than the situation seems to call for. I'll show you where your room is. *(They exit.)*

PROLOGUE. In the world of our world, it is now late afternoon, a few days later. Our new admissions are settling in. The setting autumn sun is streaming through the thinning trees on the hospital property's edge. We are in the Crossroads Psychiatric Retreat Center. We are at a pay phone in the hall.

EPILOGUE. No argument here. It's getting darker, trees are dying. A few days later, a pay phone in the hall.

Scene 2

Man is standing near a pay phone, Woman enters.

WOMAN. I need to call somebody.

MAN. I'm waiting for someone to call.

WOMAN. I'll only be a second.

MAN. What if you suddenly find something else to talk about?

WOMAN. What if your phone call never comes?

MAN. What if the place you call is filled with people you haven't talked to in years? A line of loved ones and distant cousins, lined up through the house, waiting for their chance to get on the phone and twirl their hair and talk to you?

WOMAN. What if the person you're saying is going to call wrote the number down wrong and then lost the tiny piece of paper and was lying in the first place when he said he'd call at all?

MAN. It's a she. And she'll call. Go make your second-long call somewhere else. This is for normal human use. Phone calls lasting into the minutes and hours, years of long-distance and polite chatter, trailing off into raging and expensive silences. Humanity, on the horn. Conversation.

WOMAN. So make some conversation.

MAN. I will. *(Pause.)* Nice weather I'm having. Yes, I would have to agree with myself, there. That's a nice haircut I have. Yes, thank you, it is but a sign of human civilization. Like standing up straight and not eating worms, it's not something I can really take credit for. *(Woman begins to walk away.)* And I see you wander through life in a social architecture called the family, the rubbley remains of which we build our new relations on. Yes, we do, and we use the same name and share the same features and we all move apart so as to later hold reunions. *(Woman is gone.)* Ice cream, you scream. This is how the mind works. Poorly. Around. On the ruin of the last thought. I'm glad we had this little chat. Et cetera. "Social architecture." I'm an idiot. She has nice hair. My last ruined thought.

PROLOGUE. He is certainly outgoing and verbal, certainly expectant and full of hope, standing by a phone that doesn't take incoming calls. She is walking back and forth somewhere, ingoing, unverbal, biting her nails, rethinking the last scene. But cut to the offices of the doctor and the nurse! It is morning, days later.

EPILOGUE. In a little while, we begin to depart from an earlier reality, from the original little mess of real life we built our play on. Hardly even noticeable. All the work we put into trying to improve. The lying and pretending, the rethinking, the revising into ruin. A signature move. It's only natural. If we could control life, it wouldn't be life. If we could control our likeness of it, it wouldn't be a likeness.

Scene 3

Nurse in chair, with Woman on couch. On the other side of the stage, in very separate light, Doctor is in his chair, with Man on couch.

WOMAN. He stayed waiting, I left. That's the story. I don't know. *(Pause.)* Can I leave?

NURSE. In a little. Once — I am reminded — I didn't know, either. On a train, in a dress, in the winter. Me, and the snow coming down, as if in some famous short story, into the ocean off the shore of a cold marshy land. I saw a horse, from the train. I was on my youthful way south to see if someone might marry me, a man I had already given my hand and the rest of my body to, because that's what you did when you did that in those days. Only a pony really. Are you cold? He said no, go home — essentially, get lost. That horse looked cold, standing in the middle of such a snowy and fictional-seeming winter. Or, pony. All the frozen marsh water around her. I never understood. The tall dead grasses. I assume it was a female. I was pretty. Not as pretty as you. Pretty enough, I thought, but, maybe not. What changed, I wanted to ask him. Cute, I guess you would say. No. Pretty, I was pretty when I was young. The way you are. The way you — I mean this as a compliment — will have been. Nice horsie, pretty girl.

WOMAN. Thank you. I'm sorry, can I go?

NURSE. No, dear. What I learned from all this is that I didn't learn that much. Live and learn — but not that much. *(Pause.)* We still have some time.

DOCTOR. How goes life here, too fast, too slow? Happily, lamentably, timelessly, around, not at all, so many choices — how goes it?

MAN. I saw someone, the other day. I tried to make conversation.

DOCTOR. Yes, I saw someone, once. Once, I, standing ankles-deep in a brook watching geese flying by, saw someone, once. I was thinking of the shape of a horse and trying to picture the cloud that might best represent it. Who comes along but — life is too remarkable — a woman. She was so pretty-looking, her collarbones, or, you know, clavicle, her clavicles, and so on, down the bones of her body.

I climbed out of my water, crying hello, crying hi. I proposed all sorts of things to her. She slowly declined, over the coming months. I invited her to the ocean. She said no and no and never and then, one coming month, yes. We were together for a time. She threw me a surprise party. I had a mild stroke. Everyone came. She gave me an antique train set and I was rushed to the hospital. Some people knock looking backwards as a way to live. I do not. Never did.

NURSE. I've felt a lot. As many people have. Where I distinguish myself is, I stand outside at night. I try to make new constellations out of the old stars, if there are old stars out. Sometimes it rains. Or there's sleet, or nothing. I don't know if this distinguishes myself. I remember I was so hurt. I stand there. Or I don't. Is this a lonely picture? I'm a professional. This may all seem as if it's ... I don't know. But it isn't. Unless it is. And if so, then, there you go. But all you need to know is that I, like the rest, like you, sit here with a serious history, with little and real fears and dreams, a heart and two eyes, looking out, from a body of bones, watching you and the rest of the world for some sign. See me looking at you. *(Brief pause.)* We have a little more time.

DOCTOR. I loved her and felt ugly. I grew to hate the way I walked, my stupid posture. I saw my dull reflection glaring at me from windows and mirrors, saying to me, "What are you looking at?" I asked myself, "Am I beautiful, inside?" No response, inside, except gurgling. None, without, except a different gurgling. People died. Winter and Summer Olympics passed. I slowly declined. I used to love the Butterfly, in swimming. The Downhill, in skiing. You probably don't see me as a man who loved so much. I, like everyone, was and was so for very long. Summer or winter, I cheered for everyone. I learned the stories of our nation's young athletes, their role models, subjects they failed in school, how hard they worked, and in such awful weather. I loved a lot. Instead of her. I don't know why.

NURSE. My one true love: a meaningless fling. I looked for the horse on the ride home.

DOCTOR. It wouldn't have killed me if things had been different.

MAN. My life is going to be different.

WOMAN. My life story unfurls itself before me in gleaming ripples and hopeful waves of never-ending and over-written difference.

NURSE. Yes. *(Earnestly.)* Good for you. Really, darling. *(Pause.)* I'm surprised, as I get older and people look me less and less in the eye, how nothing is ever different. It seems that the way things seem is the way they're going to stay seeming. There's that old saying: Buck teeth are buck teeth. And that other old saying: Horses always smell like horses.

WOMAN. Are those really old sayings?

NURSE. They will be, someday, if people start saying them now. *(She looks at her watch.)* Speaking of someday, we don't have any more time, for today.

MAN. You know what's probably pretty interesting, is that I don't think I've ever really —

DOCTOR. *(Interrupting.)* Hang on a sec. *(His pen appears to have run out of ink. He shakes it, vigorously. He finds another pen, has to draw scribbles with it for a moment, in order for the ink to begin running.)* There we go. *(Shaking his head, smiling.)* Ink. *(Scene ends.)*

PROLOGUE. It's evening. The cold air, dark sky, and historical stars. Faraway traffic goes unhonkingly by, with daylight savings over, the beaches uncrowded. It is past twilight. Geese are flying noisily overhead, mated for life, as the duck-hunting season opens. Houses and corporate headquarters are festively decorated, empty except for the light. 'Tis the season hardest to suffer, and better to hibernate through. So now we, to the TV room, for some television.

EPILOGUE. Winter isn't sad. You've had happy times in winter. And sad ones in summer. Life goes by year-round. People get married in sleet storms. People get cancer on soft summer evenings, sitting by the radio, looking up words in a dictionary. The wonderful world falls apart around the clock. You know this from experience, if you've ever had any. And there's nothing necessarily sad about anything. Or happy. I just wanted to make that clear. Am I making myself clear? It doesn't matter. You don't care. You're thinking about yourself. Our scene moves to the TV room.

Scene 4

Woman turns on the television. The television faces upstage.

TELEVISION. — cars with their lights on coming down Main Street, through this once darkened little town, now alight with grief. All, in a state of shock at the loss — the drowning — of the popular Williams family. The area always has a tragedy to grieve, but rarely a one as grievous as this. A family, in whole, pulled drowned from the local pond, after an evening of skating, a winter's outing undertaken too early in the season. We are all on thin ice, but, for some of us, it is even thinner. Young and old, they still wore their skates, tightly tied on to make up for their weak ankles. Whatever they wore, all those generations now are now gone; and, though this reporter understands that this would have naturally happened eventually, this reporter also understands it is tragic it happened now. One bright spot, they leave no family behind. They are survived by only their neighborhood and house. No legal battles will ensue. It's all settled. They're dead. Live, I am in Carlisle. Stay tuned for some holiday gift ideas and tips on ways to keep your car battery from freezing. Reporting for channel — (Woman turns off television. Pause. Man enters.)

MAN. Hi.

WOMAN. Well, if it isn't you.

MAN. Yup. Or, would it be, Nope. Hi.

WOMAN. Did your phone call come?

MAN. That thing doesn't take incoming phone calls, it turns out. Did you find somewhere to make yours from?

WOMAN. I decided not to call.

MAN. I feel bad.

WOMAN. It isn't your fault. It was better I didn't call. I'm glad.

MAN. Oh good. I'm glad. I still feel bad. (Pause.) Not because of anything to do with you.

WOMAN. I'm sorry.

MAN. It isn't your fault. As I think I just, you know, I don't know, I think, pretty clearly, said. Do you have change for the laundry room?

WOMAN. I might. (She begins to look for change.) Did you watch the sun go down tonight?

MAN. (Pause.) Don't you see what's happening here?

WOMAN. No.

MAN. Me neither.

WOMAN. Did you see the sunset?

MAN. Oh, right — the sun, going down. No. I didn't. I think I can honestly say, I did not.

WOMAN. You should have. It was pretty. It was cold-looking. A person could come up with all kinds of words, if he sat down and tried.

MAN. I'm sure. *(Pause.)* Bye. *(Begins to leave.)*

WOMAN. Do you have anyone come, for visiting hours?

MAN. I'm separated.

WOMAN. Is your wife near here?

MAN. Oh I'm not married. I just kind of meant —

WOMAN. Me neither.

MAN. I thought I would be divorced by now. Sometimes I see a rickety little house with broken shutters and a tiny swimming pool and I think, "I'd like to get married, and then get divorced, and then live there." But I never met the right person. See you around.

WOMAN. Didn't you need quarters?

MAN. No. No, thanks. That was just a need I had. Something to act on. And so I did. And here we are. Bye, again. *(He exits. Woman exits.)*

PROLOGUE. Do things seem aimless? Maybe that's how things are. Do you think anyone has a future? An aim? The man and woman? The Nurse and Doctor? Are you an optimist? Do you see a love scene on the sunless horizon? Are you good at making things up? And can you properly repress? My questions won't get us anywhere. My answers wouldn't either. But, so, to the Group Therapy Room, for group therapy, in the morning.

EPILOGUE. Is the main action of the play a man with a pencil in his hand, sitting at a desk in the morning, trying to come up with a word for sunset? Is the through-story *(so-called)* thrown away? As he tries to revise the play and create ornate metaphors for simple things? As the old fears creep in. The old story. Is repetition a failure in daring, or a step toward deliverance? Could be both. Don't know, never knew. So, to the Group Therapy Room, for group therapy, in the morning. I quote. Or, repeat. Because, why wouldn't I? That's what we do.

Scene 5

Doctor, Nurse, Man, Woman, are seated together.

DOCTOR. It was always one of the most beautiful places and times in the world for me.

NURSE. *(Long pause.)* What was?

DOCTOR. Didn't I say? I'm sorry. The Netherlands, when I went when I was young. The days were young girls. Blue skies, yellow flowers, the world's largest diamond. Decent drugs, Anne Frank's attic, tall blonde Dutch women on vintage bicycles, and me. I saw the King at a tennis game.

NURSE. *(Pause.)* How does traveling make people feel?

WOMAN. I've never been anywhere. No, yes I have.

MAN. Sad.

NURSE. I'm sorry?

MAN. Traveling makes me feel sad.

NURSE. Why, do you think?

MAN. Why do I *think?* I guess because —

NURSE. *(Interrupting.)* Why do you think it makes you feel sad?

MAN. I don't *think* it makes me feel sad. Traveling makes me feel sad. F, E, E, L. S, A, D.

NURSE. Oh, a speller.

DOCTOR. Maybe — M, A, Y, B, E — it has something to do with all the things going past in the window. The sadness, I mean. Life life life, mile after mile. You're a smiling baby, a reckless teen, a tax-paying adult, a corpse. Bang bang bang. You're just getting the hang of the toilet and, suddenly, time to pick out a coffin. I'm kidding. Or, exaggerating. Slightly. *(Brief pause.)* Amsterdam. *(Everyone looks at Doctor. Pause.)*

WOMAN. Once I lived a whole summer with a friend's family. I did everything they did. I got stung by bees and tried drinking and simple kinds of kissing. It was hard being away and then hard being home. Is that something like what you were looking for someone to say?

NURSE. Just like, dear. Thank you. I guess we're all away from somewhere. Away from some house on some street, or from some position in relation to the body of the mother. By dint of our being here. Did anyone know that "dintless" was a word?

MAN. Did anyone ever see a movie called "By Dint of the Bridge's Collapse?"

WOMAN. Is that where the shoe-shine boy is always staring at the girl who sells flowers? But there's no reason to buy flowers and no one has good shoes because the whole town is totally poor and sad. He's a poet. Or he's thinking about it. The girl only eats vitamins.

DOCTOR. And she was played by Susette de Baronelle, who I was a little in love with. Still a little am.

NURSE. Movies are wonderful. I didn't see that particular one.

MAN. And his brother keeps bringing different animals home and naming them all the same thing. And, right, the main boy stares at the main girl. You never know if they ever meet, or ever fall in love. The town is in a sort of quarantine.

DOCTOR. *(Looking at his watch and his notepad.)* I know this has only been a few pages, but we have to stop. *(He takes out an appointment book.)* Sorry. Funny, life. We don't even have time to misrepresent ourselves. We hardly have time to make a tragic error of our lives. Oh, well; ah, well. Now, before everyone leaves, I need to change next week. *(He begins writing in appointment book and, as he's writing, says, off-handedly:)* I'm starting to think it was Belgium I went to, and that I only read about Amsterdam.

PROLOGUE. The weeks change anyway. Another little pause in the world. *(Pause. Perhaps Prologue turns around to survey the quiet stage.)* Then, right on cue, here comes more time, giving us life, rushing past, taking it away. Time. Do you feel it? Ladies and gentlemen, do you? It's there. I wouldn't know how it feels. In words. That's all right. It's late on an early winter's evening, and we, to the rec. room, rush!

EPILOGUE. In other words: tick-tock, tick-tock. But, again, well-enough said. "The weeks change anyway." Time is important here, to us. The general sweep of it, not its particularities. "Sweep" is the wrong word, but, you'll live with it. Gentle, deadly. Slow and violent, it just goes by. I wouldn't look for some life-changing event. Except life, or illness, or death. This is all supposed to be at least plausible, after all, our play. Real American realism. But, so, what changed your life? Forever. Whatever it was, it's probably still doing it. Tick, tock. Or to put it another way, at what moment did your life suddenly stay the same forever. It's night in the rec. room. We claim. You're sitting there in the dark. Strangers, forever, on either side.

Scene 6

Man is assembling a balsa-wood toy airplane. Woman walks by in the background, upstage. She stops to look and listen, unseen. Perhaps, it is in this moment that she begins to fall in love with him.

MAN. All quiet, as I assemble a balsa-wood toy airplane. I'll use a rubber band to drive the propeller. Once finished, once this project of mine is done, when the little toy can finally fly, it won't help anything, but it will fly beautifully and sputteringly high above this dirt-bound life, without changing anything, and then crash, without end, until it's over. *(Woman exits.)*

PROLOGUE. Night's over. And it's morning. And we return to rooms we thought we left. We return to the rec. room. It makes you wonder. Have we already been through all the rooms? Have life and the whole world already been written — been foreseen, foretold, long been forborne? Is the ending of the story already in your bones? The fevered climax already long in your cold blood?

EPILOGUE. Maybe. Probably. But you hope that along the way there will still be, sometimes, a surprise. We're back in the rec. room, yes. The woman enters, yelling:

Scene 7

WOMAN. Surprise! *(She enters holding a lit candle. The balsa-wood airplane is completed. She sings.)* Happy Birthday to You. *(She speaks.)* You know the middle part. *(She sings the final line.)* Happy Birthday to You. *(She speaks.)* I guess you know the ending, too. The fevered climax is probably already long in your cold blood. But it seemed unkind somehow, or anti-art, not to sing it.

MAN. My birthday isn't until spring.

WOMAN. How would I know that? We've hardly talked. That's what makes this so gracious an act. So mysterious.

MAN. It is pretty gracious an act. Pretty mysterious. Thanks. *(He holds up the candle.)* Was there a cake that came with this?

WOMAN. My uncle died on his birthday last year.

MAN. I'm sorry. He's in a better place, I guess.

WOMAN. We don't know. He had a nice house. A garden. He died.

MAN. I'm sorry.

WOMAN. It's not your fault. Is it? It isn't. His gravestone read, "Here lies the late myself, dead as far as the eye can see."

MAN. Cake? *(He feeds her an imaginary piece of cake.)*

WOMAN. Mmmm. Not bad. Here, you. *(She feeds him a piece.*

Pause.) You put your hand in my mouth, just then.

MAN. Ditto you yours in mine.

WOMAN. What a cold and intriguing sentence. I remember, once, I don't know why I remember — oh, I know why: it was cold. And intriguing. To me. But, so, up north, once, I threw all this outdoor furniture off the roof of a museum. Chairs and tables and glass ashtrays. That was the start of my adulthood. I was trying to become a lifeguard. I was supposed to be rescuing things. Around that point, people stopped returning my calls, generally. I started acting really psychological. When I bled — you know, girl stuff — I bled too much.

MAN. Oh. A lot of that kind of went over my — so, did you ever become a lifeguard? Wasn't the water cold up there? I got really emotional next to a screen door, once. So there was that. *(Pause.)* Have you seen outside? It looks like rain. Or snow.

WOMAN. What does?

MAN. It does, what else, the — I don't know — sky, the firmament. The, um, welkin. We pretended to eat pretend-cake. I find that sort of interesting. We shared something that doesn't exist and that, no matter how much we want it to, never ever —

WOMAN. *(Interrupting.)* It was interesting. I'm looking forward to seeing you again.

MAN. Are you leaving?

WOMAN. No. It was for children, I should add.

MAN. What was? The museum was?

WOMAN. I should go.

MAN. Did I say something?

WOMAN. Did it sound to you as if you said something? I didn't hurt anyone, throwing the stuff off. Even though I broke everything. And could have killed someone. I feel as if I should go. And that usually means I should go. Bye. *(Exits.)*

MAN. Bye. *(To himself.)* I feel as if I should go. *(Scene ends.)*

PROLOGUE. Despite winter coming at these two from every angle and direction, one can sense a little spring in their speech. Them two, warming toward each other. Our scene moves ahead one week. And it has snowed. And it is night. On the grounds, somebody built six snowmen, facing different ways, standing too close together. And our love story has progressed without us. Will we catch up to it, overtake it? Either way, to the sunroom, in the moonlight.

EPILOGUE. The birthday scene was a happy scene. But let's not be precious. It wasn't even anyone's birthday. And if not these two

24

talking, then two others. Or one of them and someone else, some third person. The history of plays and the history of the world is a set of the same conversations being had by different people. We've all been through them. "You are the only one, forever," we swear, having sworn it twice, or more. People are liars, but, liars are people. Take me. I'm an excellent example. So, forgive and forget. Then die and be forgotten. Or, I don't know — maybe there's more to it. But in the meantime these two are becoming sort of lovely together. I admit. A handsome couple. Either way, we are in the sun room. A week later, a night, the Winter Solstice.

Scene 8

Nurse and Doctor are seated, wearing winter jackets. They have skates. There is a bowl of plastic fruit on the table before them.

NURSE. They're probably having one of their very particular conversations, in which they both take such solace. I remember those conversations, those whispered times — so original, such pure meaning and total motivation, you know? You go ahead. I'll wait.
DOCTOR. No, no. I'll wait with you. It'll make the time go by faster. *(Long pause. The time doesn't go by faster. They fidget.)* I haven't skated in a while.
NURSE. How about that heartbreaking story of that family skating. And the ice broke and they all fell through? Williams, was it? The name?
DOCTOR. I think, yes. Imagine, a dead family. When they dragged the bodies out, the whole town could hardly keep staring. I thought I might speak about it, might try to bang it up into words, at the conference on the National Grief in the spring. To the which, by the way, I would, I must say, of course — it goes without saying — love you to come.
NURSE. Please, Doctor. Must you be so forward?
DOCTOR. I'm sorry, you're right. There was a lot of punctuation in that invitation. But it would be wonderful and helpful. Give it some thought. Period. Speeches about grief during the day, a whirlpool, a shower, and then cocktails at seven. It's in one of those

little sea towns. We could take the train down.

NURSE. I haven't been to the ocean since I was a girl. I was a girl at one time, Doctor, as you are probably aware.

DOCTOR. We could play golf. Doctors are pretty good at golf. I never played. Don't tell anyone, I could lose my license. And I was aware.

NURSE. I would love to see the sun set over somewhere different.

DOCTOR. So it's decided. Is it decided? Well, you think, and then decide.

NURSE. I will.

DOCTOR. *(Looking at the bowl of fruit. Offhandedly:)* These are fake, I just noticed. *(Man and Woman enter.)*

NURSE. And here they are! Come on, you two. Everyone is waiting.

WOMAN. You go ahead. I'm cold. I want to put on more clothes.

DOCTOR. Okay, but quickly now. Time's a-wasting. There's only so much cocoa. That's my philosophy.

NURSE. You can't go wrong with a philosophy like that. Also, "Don't get sick in Europe," someone once told me. *(To Man.)* You need a hat. And hurry. We're going to light some sparklers. *(Nurse and Doctor exit.)*

WOMAN. Let's stay. I've seen a sparkler before.

MAN. Okay. Are you thinking what I'm thinking?

WOMAN. Are you thinking about when I burned my hand one year on New Year's Eve?

MAN. No.

WOMAN. Then no.

MAN. You look pretty.

WOMAN. Maybe I am pretty.

MAN. That would explain it. *(Pause.)* Where were you hiding yourself today?

WOMAN. In the basement, behind the hot-water heater.

MAN. You missed exercise this morning.

WOMAN. I said I was under the weather. And behind the hot-water heater. I always liked exercise.

MAN. I bet you throw like a girl.

WOMAN. I am a girl.

MAN. Oh, hello. Are your mother and father still together?

WOMAN. My father is. *(Brief pause.)* But don't change subjects so fast. Because, just don't, please. Swimming is an interest I have. Let's talk about that. "What Swimming Is Like." Begin. Discuss. Enlarge. You have an average lifetime.

MAN. Swimming is different. From walking.

WOMAN. I see.

MAN. It's fun.

WOMAN. I see. Go on.

MAN. I'll never be how you think.

WOMAN. Oh.

MAN. Whales swim.

WOMAN. They do. Every day of the week.

MAN. There's enough room in the ocean for everyone in the world to have room to drown in. Do you see? *(He looks at the ceiling, speaks quickly.)* But don't leave me, don't leave me, *(She moves to his side.)* please don't leave me, please —

WOMAN. *(She interrupts. Puts her hand on his shoulder.)* Here I am, I'm right here —

MAN. *(He interrupts. Unkindly. He shrugs her hand off.)* Listen, can't you see I'm in the middle of something?

NURSE. *(Enters.)* I forgot my scarf. Come on, you two. Don't just sit around here and miss everything. Okay, Miss Everything? *(She playfully flicks Woman with her scarf.)* And Mister Everything Else. The world is racing by and Doctor is skating around backward. He also just proposed to me that we all build an igloo. Does my hair look okay? Do I look, would you say, crazed, at all? Anyway, hurry. *(Exits.)*

MAN. I'm sorry I yelled.

WOMAN. You didn't yell. *(Pause.)* I don't want to miss everything. I really don't. I like everything.

MAN. Me neither. *(Pause.)* I meant to yell.

WOMAN. *(Pause.)* Name a season.

MAN. Winter.

WOMAN. Name another.

MAN. Spring.

WOMAN. We were made for each other.

MAN. Name an animal.

WOMAN. The otter.

MAN. Name another.

WOMAN. No thanks.

MAN. We were.

WOMAN. Can we go be alone somewhere?

MAN. Both of us?

WOMAN. Yeah.

MAN. I know just the place.

WOMAN. Where?

MAN. I don't know, I've just heard people say that before.

WOMAN. How about your room?

MAN. If you don't mind the state it's in.

WOMAN. No.

MAN. And you don't mind that it's mine.

WOMAN. No.

MAN. Or that everything in it is mine. If you don't mind that loss shall be yours. And then even that will be taken away. And it might be messy. Are you allergic to dust?

WOMAN. No.

MAN. I want you to have the last word.

WOMAN. *(Pause.)* Sympathy? *(They exit, him carrying her.)*

PROLOGUE. What more could anyone want? What would anyone add? And why? And how would he phrase it? *(Brief pause.)* I'll say this. Their skin is young. And they know nothing. Unlike ourselves, whose skin is old and who know nothing. But onward. There is no need to show what we all can so easily imagine, what we also all so often and easily imagine. For instance, her taking his hand in hers and running it over her mouth, wetting it, running it over each breast, to down between her legs where all of herself comes together. All in a single fluid movement. And then him responding in kind, whispering into her eye, gently pulling her hair. They both say, "God." They both come to an understanding. And it's over. They lie all over each other. *(Pause.)* Now it's late. The skaters have all come in. What cocoa is left over is frozen. The doctor fell and sprained his ankle, having fun and showing off. Nobody drowned. Winter has officially begun. Somebody lost a mitten. It's quiet and nothing more need be said.

EPILOGUE. Probably not. Probably not. *(Pause.)* But, feelings between the man and woman, yes. The two characters seem right, beside the other, like the character of the bird and the rock in ancient Chinese writing, beside the other. One bird, one stone. What is between the man and the woman is starting to seem inevitable, as with the rock and the bird. Will they be beside themselves forever? Do you follow my drift? From away from where we were? Is it noticeable yet? For I have one, a drift. All will painfully make itself painfully clear. Oh, but for now, such splendor, the liquid movements, the responding in kind, the hair, the hands, my God. Almost makes you ... *(He stares off, wistfully. Returns abruptly.)* I don't know. The room of the man.

Scene 9

MAN. Do you see children anywhere on your horizon? A little baby screaming out of you? A new father standing frozen in horror behind his rented video equipment, trying to smile and focus? And a new voice in the world, crying? A new cry. Is that so crazy-sounding?

WOMAN. No.

MAN. How about: Once I was younger with legs unbroken and dreams undreamt, years before I'd met or left anyone, a sister in a snowsuit to my right, the King of the Dutch above, and now to the future, my mouth on you, parting the ocean and your legs, baying at the moon and earth, crying, "Mother Mother," or "Not Mother, Not Mother," crying, "Writing." Crying, nothing. Wanting only to be lonely and home, to be drenched on the inside with blood, as usual, waiting, a man in a house, this is my vision, et cetera, so let slip the dogs of love and talk among yourself while I go change into something less promising. *(Pause.)* Is *that* so crazy-sounding?

WOMAN. A little. But I could see a child. We could take family trips to the beach. You would look for a place for our towel. I would pull my suit down from where it had ridden up. Us, on the world, sunburned, hungry — a little family. Taking showers under those little weak showers that they have in front of the giant ocean. And something to eat, after. Also, lowering your fly while we're driving home. A wet road map. The baby, asleep. Showering at home. You have pretty bones in your face. I would always lose my keys. You could type upstairs. Is this too scattered-sounding?

MAN. No.

PROLOGUE. Ah, love.

WOMAN. You should have the last word.

MAN. *(Nurse and Doctor enter at other side of stage, but remain in a separate playing area from Man and Woman.)* Sympathy is such a good one. But let's see. Ocean, no; Medication, no; Redemption, no; Cocoa, no; Myself, no; Salvation, no; It isn't Summer, Trust, or Honesty, no. It's from Latin I have a feeling. I don't know. Dire? Is dire Latin? Is "Latin" Latin? *(Man and Woman exit.)*

NURSE. I think it's beautiful.

DOCTOR. It's a little unheard of, isn't it? I never heard of anything like this. I fear for them.

NURSE. I'm sure they fear for themselves just fine.

DOCTOR. How far have things progressed? If I may use so clinical a term. See, there's the problem. A growing clinicality. The old heart-breaking songs don't break my heart anymore. I haven't cried for the last five presidents. But, how far?

NURSE. Far, I imagine, from the distant look they give each other. Those old songs will break your heart again, or the new ones will, when they're old. *(Pause.)* I saw people ice-fishing, driving in this morning. There was a little bird flying over all the holes. How is your ankle healing?

DOCTOR. Correctly, I think, I thank you. I'm glad it's not broken. You'd have to carry me all over that conference.

NURSE. Which I would do with a smile. A grimace, I guess. A sort of pained, burdened, hyperventilating but not unhappy grimace. A smile.

PROLOGUE. Outside the window, a kite in a tree is covered in ice. People's bodies looked changed in the distance of the parking lot — hunched, closed, as seen in ultrasound — as they struggle with their frozen car door locks. Something to behold. And how long can they be beheld? How long can an image be kept in mind? I wouldn't hold your breath. Go stretch. I need to relieve myself. We'll take a little break, an intermission. Please come back, and, if you do, maybe you'll find that the cushion of your seat is cold and has given up the shape that you gave it, that there is no trace of you but your absence and a few gum wrappers. No trace. Imagine that. Hard to conceive. Almost impossible for us to conceive. See you soon.

EPILOGUE. *(He stands as if about to deliver a soliloquy, seeming to be considering many things.)* Fifteen minutes. *(Lights down.)*

ACT TWO

Scene 1

Lights up on Man and Woman, seated next to each other, but not touching. They stay very still. Lights down. They exit.

PROLOGUE. You've come back. Some time passed, in the last few minutes. Christmas did. Life continued. Christmas ended. Those decorations that made it through the wind and cold unbroken now are all down and put away. Whatever was frozen, froze harder. On the south lawn are snow forts and snow angels losing their child-made form. Very very north of here, a polar bear is eating a seal cub. And far over that, a dead satellite launched from Florida, America, during an earlier presidency, is floating out of control in freezing outer space. Back on Earth, we are in the reading room, in the Common Era.

EPILOGUE. What if you were writing a play and your feelings changed? You didn't even know how you felt anymore, or what you thought. You couldn't keep going. The image disintegrated. Your mind wasn't up to it, or your heart. Would your claim to realism be lost if you didn't somehow incorporate the change, the not-knowing, the cold feeling? Even if only subtly? Would you just abort the whole thing? Wash your hands of the whole bloody mess? What would you do, back on Earth? If this were you? *(Pause.)* We move our scene to the reading room, sure, why not, in the Common Era.

Scene 2

Lights up on Man and Woman. He is reading.

WOMAN. Where were you yesterday?

MAN. I had to take some tests.

WOMAN. What kind of tests, blood tests? History tests?

MAN. I took a Spielberger Rage and Anger Index, a Van Beck Depression Composite, a Taylor Manifest Anxiety Scale, and, just out of curiosity, a Minnesota Multiphasic Personality Inventory.

WOMAN. *(Pause.)* How did they go?

MAN. I think I did really well.

WOMAN. *(Pause.)* What are you reading?

MAN. The dictionary.

WOMAN. How is it?

MAN. You know the joke. It's a little wordy. The verbs are good, at the beginning. You get sick of them.

WOMAN. I'll wait for the movie. *(Pause.)* You don't think that's funny?

MAN. Listen to this, *(He reads.)* "Hilaktia: Disorder named for Greek ruler whose vivid nightmares of winter caused him to die and his body to manifest all signs of having frozen, despite the season being summer, the weather being warm. He wrote several plays, which survive in fragments or not at all. The disorder is characterized by a flight of ideas, a fear of the mind, and disregard for language; also paleness and change, hatred. Treatable, with bright light, photographs, medicative therapies."

WOMAN. *(Pause.)* What am I supposed to think about that?

MAN. You got me. Something, though. You'd think you'd think something. *(Pause.)* Don't you ever change clothes? I'm sorry I said that. But don't you? Forget I said that. Forget I said I'm sick of you and your body and sick of our story. One side of me seems to say — I don't know. Forget it. Listen to me, my sucky vocabulary. Blah! Blahhh! I wonder if I have that General's disease. Or, whatever, "ruler."

WOMAN. Maybe you just need —

MAN. *(Interrupting.)* Thanks, I'll try that.

PROLOGUE. Do you remember somebody mentioning an otter? When verb followed noun, when the man and woman spoke lovingly and plainly in simple yups and good old household nopes? The beautiful woman said — it was such a beautiful line — "Yes." I forget what the beautiful man had asked her. I forget the exact feeling. But I can say the word beautiful. I could say a lot of words, if I sat down and tried. And I do know where this is going. So, to someplace! Lights, action!

EPILOGUE. Darkness, inaction. As an aside, have you ever been stung by a bee that had nothing against you? Or bitten by a dog who otherwise seemed to like you? Or fell, due to a gravity not your own? Or hurt someone you loved, or used to love, or never did? Ever suffer loss? Ever slowly lose control of something? Ever slowly lose control of everything? Fail? Ever fucking really badly fail?

Scene 3

WOMAN. Interesting people have interesting names. This is sort of a juncture. For us. Would getting one of those books of children's names be a good idea?

MAN. Theoretically.

WOMAN. You have to have some feelings. Name some names.

MAN. Lawyer Malloy. Bodhisattva. Steve Stevenson, I don't know. I think Alexander Graham Bell has a certain ring to it.

WOMAN. A first name will be fine. And what if she's a girl?

MAN. Then you can name her You, after you. Or, I don't know. Simone? Isn't there a human name, Simone?

WOMAN. Please, darling, try.

MAN. All right, darling, I will.

WOMAN. Now, think.

MAN. I'm thinking. *(Pause.)* I've thought. *(Pause.)* I should speak. This might hurt. *(Pause.)* What if there is someone else?

WOMAN. There's everyone else.

MAN. No, no there isn't. What if I don't care about this, because I'm in love with someone else. That would be quite a turn. The famous, "another woman." What if. She studied trumpet and she's teaching me the harmonica. We play in the snow. I gave her the children's book you gave me that I said I had lost.

33

WOMAN. I'm sorry? I'm preoccupied with the baby, yours, inside of me. You said something about a trumpet?

MAN. I said something about my lying and cheating and going back on my word. Listen to this, the following words: my feelings changed. From away from ones of love.

WOMAN. Stop it.

MAN. I already did. It'll be as if I never started. I would have told you sooner, but, I don't know.

WOMAN. You're serious.

MAN. Not really. I don't know. I am.

WOMAN. What is her name?

MAN. Again, with names. You wouldn't believe me if I told you.

WOMAN. Why not?

MAN. Because I'd be lying.

EPILOGUE. Ah, love.

WOMAN. *(Pause.)* How could you do this?

MAN. This? Is that how you would denote my million million feelings: "this?" Or do I mean "connote?"

WOMAN. Just the other day we were talking —

MAN. *(Interrupting.)* I know I keep interrupting, but, "The Other Day and The Other Day and The Other Day. Life is but a bucket boy drumming for loose change, a person playing pots and pans on the street as a way to get some food. Or, not really, not at all. That isn't at all what life was, The Other Day, The Other Day, The Other Day." It ends a little weakly, kind of tails off, but how's that for a soliloquy?

WOMAN. Please listen. Just to this one little thing. I want you to listen. When I was little, before school or anything — *(Brief pause.)* You gave her the book I brought back from England? I walked forever. I went through miles of stupid English rain to buy that stupid book. I loved that stupid book. *Sleepy Time Rhymes.* We colored it together. And you gave it away to some bitch to remain unnamed?

MAN. Don't swear. I hate swearing. When you hear swearing you know the person has lost the feeling. But, that book, I believe you mentioned that book, *Sleepy Time Rhymes.* It made her happy. She loved it, too. She cried over it. We read it to each other and went through it with White-Out and uncolored it. It was our best night.

WOMAN. What did I do?

MAN. Nothing. Somewhere, though, someone did something. It

would seem. Once, there was a pretty pretty girl. Maybe she's the one who did something. Time will take care of her. We'll see what pretty bones her face is made up of. Her, I loved. Unlike you and the woman I'm now leaving you for. Her name is Margaret, too.

WOMAN. My name's not Margaret.

MAN. No, I know. I just meant that she's another person with that name.

PROLOGUE. Welcome to a play whose — *Parlez-vous Anglais? Sprechen Sie Englisch? Niwappi inglappa? Schones totes Kind, estos zapatos son cuellos? Esti palid. Mimi niliyeona nasema hivi. Wo est der Zoo?* I speak English. Or, I used to. We now rejoin — This doesn't cohere. I can't make this make sense. *(He exits.)*

EPILOGUE. He just said, "Welcome to a play whose — Do you speak English? Do you speak English? Do you speak English? Beautiful dead child, whose shoes are those? You are pale. I who saw say thus. Where is the zoo? I speak English. Or, I used to. We now rejoin — This doesn't cohere. I can't make this make sense." I quote. For what it's worth. Which is probably very little. But maybe not. I'm not big on assigning values. But, it's entertaining to see people in pain, yes? *(He looks to where Prologue has just exited.)* We now rejoin the man and the woman. It doesn't matter where.

Scene 4

WOMAN. You can stop loving me overnight?

MAN. I started loving you overnight.

WOMAN. We took walks. We undressed each other. You said such beautiful true-sounding things.

MAN. Get lost. *(He returns to reading the dictionary.)* "Should. Verb. Origin unknown. Used to express duty, obligation, necessity." *(He has mistakenly read "used to" as meaning "formerly did" rather than "employed to.")* What? Oh, *used* to, I see. *(Pause. Doctor enters.)* Say, what do you think we should name the baby?

DOCTOR. Did you both forget? Everyone's going out on the hill for a big photograph. We're losing daylight, so rush. We need everyone. I would come back if I could. I heard you fighting.

MAN. Just she was fighting.

DOCTOR. One person can't fight.

35

WOMAN. Yes one can. I was, just. Me, alone, fighting.

DOCTOR. I'm wrong again, then. Malpractice, my old friend. But let's go outside. We never get good weather, so let's not let it blow over. Winter is going to kill everything and we want to have a photograph to look at to keep us warm while we suffer through it. I know this is a bad time, but it's for the Crossroads brochure. *(Woman, Man, and Doctor exit.)*

PROLOGUE. *(He enters. His hair is messed up, his clothes are disheveled. He has a glass of water.)* I apologize for the awful languages that I was using before. It's just that … I don't know. Sometimes we don't … *(Pause. He regains some composure. Is resigned to continue on.)* Anyway. They all go. They stare at the camera. Like life, it's over, like that. Long complicated life histories, over, click. Where did all the talk about the ocean go? Down some drain, out to sea? And you? How are you? Think of yourself when you were younger. Did you ever love anybody? I bet you did. You looked so proud. Your nice shoes and clothes are still somewhere. Maybe you're thinking of that. As you live on, as you lose some more of the rest of your life quietly, wrecking yourself in the dark. I don't know. *(Pause.)* Everybody leaves. The photographer gets in his car. Day is over again.

EPILOGUE. Right. Right. One more thing. There's more snow in the forecast, moving in like a hungry animal from somewhere out over the ocean. If you'll forgive me the simile. Which you probably don't. So I take it back. It's black, out. The freezing shitty night settles. I've lost the feeling. This is useless. I don't care about the time or where anyone is.

Scene 5

Woman, Man, and Doctor enter. A pause, almost a minute long. They stand, not knowing exactly where they should be, as neither narrator has set the scene.

NURSE. *(Enters.)* Good morning, everyone. *(Pause.)* I see our scene has moved to the group therapy room, for group therapy. *(They all move across stage and seat themselves.)* Did someone get

36

sick in the hallway?

WOMAN. Is this an experience experienced by anyone? Where it's just you and someone, and you lay and lie and lie in a room. This someone is lying next to you in the breathing dark but he doesn't know who he is, and that makes you start to slip. And you make the statement: I am not in control of my body or my mind. And you state the question: So then what is the "I" that is the subject of the assertion. And then you tender the inquisition: Who is the liar, the breather, the nobody, lying next to me? And who is the one lying inside me, kicking? You won't recall this time in your life with any warmth. And you feel sick. And as you suffer all that and grow great with mistakes, you can't even count on anyone to be — not even faithful — but just humane? Just at least recognizable? Anyone? Any goddamn body? I never swear.

DOCTOR. Why doesn't everybody take a few deep breaths and —

WOMAN. *(Interrupting.)* Why doesn't everybody not do that. I've breathed deeply enough, thank you. I think I'll go be sick again. That would be the most expressive thing I could do. Words. *(She gets up, seeming light-headed.)* Excuse me. I'm sorry. I'll be all right. Or I'm wrong. I'm sorry and I won't be all right. And I'm not sorry. *(She walks downstage, stares at the audience for a moment. Perhaps she is thinking and feeling, "It is your need for plays that is causing all this to happen, that is causing me all this pain. Are you happy now?" Then she exits.)*

DOCTOR. Why don't I go see if I can say anything. *(He exits.)*

NURSE. *(Long pause. Not unkindly.)* Well. You seem to be living with yourself. I don't know exactly what to say. *(Pause.)* It's supposed to be a beautiful sunset, tomorrow night. Or the night after that. Or that's what they said. Why don't we ... I should ... *(Nurse exits. Man exits.)*

PROLOGUE. Traffic lights are changing, clicking, alone across the suburbs, the tundras, the empty urban intersections. I'm picturing this and telling you this. I don't know why.

EPILOGUE. Click, click. Tick, tock. This last night is now weeks ago. A new routine has set in. We are in evening. The action moves to a waiting room. Enjoy.

Scene 6

WOMAN. *(Lights up. She is sitting, staring into the audience. Pause. Lights down.)*
EPILOGUE. And to a laundry room.

Scene 7

MAN. *(Lights up. He is sitting, staring into the audience. Pause. Lights down.)*
EPILOGUE. And to an office.

Scene 8

DOCTOR. She says she'll take care of the child. She keeps saying, "Me and the world will carry on." Then she looks at a lamp or a pile of books and says, "Won't we, world?" It makes you want to cry to hear.
NURSE. He says he never did well when people tested his personality. Then he says, "This is just a stage." Then he doesn't say anything. Except, then he says, "Everything will end, happily." The comma makes me worry. I listen and nod and say something I've said before.
DOCTOR. And then there's me. I stand here, idly. An empty white coat, a dry pen in my pocket. My oath is to first do no harm. But I don't do anything, ever. Except this. I stand outside and tilt my head and listen to the traffic and wonder if it's people coming or people going and revel at how it all sounds the same. Is that a promising entrance or heartbreaking exit? Then, like everyone, I go make notes, enter a journal entry on a scrap of paper to be left behind or recycled. Maybe I doodle a little design, heave a heavy — I don't know — sigh. I'm glad you're here. I've told you my

hobby. What do you like to do?

NURSE. I'm glad you're here. Everything will quiet down eventually. I'm too busy for hobbies. Except reading and skiing and landscape painting, quilting, modern dance, tennis, calligraphy, comparative philology, and astronomy. I'm kidding. I thought a little levity might … I think I'd like listening to the traffic. *(Pause.)* Spring will be pretty, the birds and the bees, and your speaking engagement. Then of course you'll have to decide how you're going to injure and embarrass yourself in the inter-hospital softball game. *(They share a little laugh.)*

PROLOGUE. Ah, finally, kindness. Love is deep and real and everywhere. All is well and all will be even better. We can see this all around us, clearly.

EPILOGUE. What a pain. I'm sick of the story. I'm sick of you. Next scene. It's got flowers in it.

Scene 9

Woman is asleep in bed. Nurse enters with flowers.

NURSE. Here are some flowers, dear.

WOMAN. *(She is waking.)* Was I, What did I … I was in a field that went down to this water. Everyone was watching me. I looked nice. Someone wrote "You're cold" on my arm. I wanted to thank everyone for being —

NURSE. *(Interrupting.)* Hello, darling. Easy, slowly. It was just a dream. I know it's hard. It gets harder and more awful, but it never ceases being beautiful. Or this is made up, and I'm lying. Either way, I brought you some flowers.

WOMAN. Could I brush my hair?

NURSE. I remember wanting to do the exact same thing. After I underwent this same procedure — an abortion, not to put too fine a point on it. I was to remain an unwed non-mother. *(Man appears at the door.)* And who is that young man, so boyishly entering. I'll leave you two alone. Yell, if it gets too lonely. *(She exits.)*

MAN. They said you were sick.

WOMAN. How kind of them to phrase it that way.

MAN. Is there anything I can get? *(Pause.)* Is it contagious?

WOMAN. No. I had them evacuate the fetal material attached to my uterine wall. Can you think up a better name for that? A girl's name? There are so many pretty ones. *(She closes her eyes. Doctor and Nurse enter. Prologue leaves his narrator's position to join them. Nurse is holding a sweater. Doctor has a tray of food. Prologue has a heart-shaped box of candy. One by one, they set these things down, on a table or at the foot of the bed, and exit. Prologue returns downstage to where he narrates from. She opens her eyes.)* That was nice of everyone. You know, it physically hurt. It still really physically does. You don't know. Once, sweat from you got in my eye. It physically burned and I liked it. Will this be going into your play? And do you wonder whether you'll allow me to recover? What would be your name for this? This procedure, you and I, our life? I should go. But I don't think I can walk. So, you. Come on, go. Consider yourself forgiven, your almost pretty eyes forgotten. Hand me that candy, please. I will be polite up to the end. I was never a person who swore, even though you had me swearing. Please go. No, wait. *(Pause.)* Now go. *(Man exits.)*

PROLOGUE. I — I wish — Now we — The — *(Pause.)* I could misquote the old books. That might be meaningful. *What flowers could grow out of this rocky garbage? A gross of broken statues and a pile of overdue books. Maybe the thunder will say something motherly.* Maybe someone will say something kind.

EPILOGUE. *(He steps a step forward, pauses, a tiny shrug. He lowers his head, slightly, and steps back.)*

PROLOGUE. *(Pause. He is holding a photograph.)* Here is the picture from the hill that everyone stood on. You can see their breath. Aren't pictures of people beautiful. But, our story! Our scene moves up the coast, to the dazzling, cold, and pacific Atlantic Ocean! Quickly! To a young family, in the sun, happily. With all speed, fly! *(The scene does not change. It is Woman in bed, still.)*

EPILOGUE. Oops.

Scene 10

WOMAN. *(She is taking sleeping pills, one with each sentence or so.)* This little piggy went to market. This little piggy is not careful. This little piggy's bladder relaxes, as she wets herself, as she did when she was little. And someone blew my house down. I was trusting, *Mein*

40

Schones totes Kind. I will huff and puff and die. *Uff-hay* and *uff-pay*, in Pig Latin. *Ipso facto*, in regular non-Pig Latin. I am killing my body, in English. I knew everything. Dad? Tell me the story of me. A sleepy time rhyme. Italicize my life. This little. *(She closes her eyes.)* PROLOGUE. *(He stares at the scene of Woman in bed. He turns to the audience, pauses. Begins to open his mouth. Closes it.)* EPILOGUE. Stop crying. Practice holding and kissing your pillow, for when the day comes you really need to hold and kiss it. This is what I tell myself, softly. There's a philosophy for you. Or, for me. And don't get sick in Europe. Life is a word game. I don't know what else. *(Pause.)* Everything is worse, including our desire for improvement. Of a life, a life story, a play. All are awful, worse, the same, but, in the end, to be lived with. Life is fine. It's spring. In fatigue and a lack of creativity, we fall back on the device of a telephone.

Scene 11

DOCTOR. *(He is speaking on the telephone.)* I would like you to come down. I need to speak with you about your daughter. *(Pause.)* I would like to speak to you in person. Here. *(Pause.)* Please come. I'm sorry for being difficult. Thank you. *(Pause.)* I really need to speak with you, here. Person-to-person is best. Yes, a right turn after the big wooden ice cream cone. Thank you. *(He hangs up the telephone.)* EPILOGUE. *(Pause. Looks over at Prologue, who stares into the audience.)* Nothing to say? Cat got your tongue, and the rest of your body? No more scribbley poetry to throw at the moment? Lost your nerve? Can't do it? The image, disintegrated, a pile of cold synonyms. I guess I understand. I guess I remember, too. *(To audience.)* It is weeks later, again. Spring, more flowers. A desk. Sunlight. A patient sits near the desk with his belongings in a bag marked "Patient's Belongings."

Scene 12

NURSE. *(She is filling out paperwork. Man is watching.)* Isn't it amazing how I can write upside-down like this? We're going to miss you. Do you have a forwarding address?

MAN. I do, but I don't know it yet. Is the doctor coming in, today?

NURSE. He said he'd try. Do you have any nice plans?

MAN. I'm so sorry. One minute, I was so sure, I completely felt as if I —

EPILOGUE. *(Interrupting. He does not believe that Man should be given the chance to explain himself or apologize.)* Outside —

MAN. I felt as if I —

EPILOGUE. *(Interrupting.)* Outside —

MAN. I wish that I —

EPILOGUE. *(Interrupting.)* Outside, it's afternoon. Clouds, sun, whatever you like. A pretty May day, too late for excuses. Carry on.

NURSE. Did you want to say something, dear?

MAN. Should I say that I was ... I don't know. What should I say? I never knew.

NURSE. Yes, dear, of course you didn't. I know. *(Pause.)* If you get out to Concord, say hello for me. Get down to that wonderful bridge they have. I went there once with a beau. We had quite a time of it down in the weeds by the water. It's one of life's wonders how pretty it is. The river going by, people going by us, us saying to each other, "Sshh, Quiet" while our lives and those people went quietly by. Oh, the daffodils, and all the other flowers, all so prettily named.

MAN. I'll try to go. *(Doctor enters walking with a cane. His face is swollen, perhaps bandaged. He has trouble speaking.)*

NURSE. Well if it isn't you.

DOCTOR. Yub. Or, whood id be, nobe? Hi. *(He is trying to say: "Yup. Or, would it be, nope? Hi.")*

NURSE. How are we today, Doctor Oh-So-Wonderfully-Handsome?

DOCTOR. Nod bad, thang you. *["Not bad, thank you.]*

MAN. Doctor, what happened?

DOCTOR. I wath looging for my trhain thet in the attig and I god thtung by beez. I broak my toe drying to ghet away from thehm. Thirdy five bee thtings in one segond, they thaid. I cand feel one thide. Bud, ind warth my band thide, ainway. *["I was looking for my train set in the attic and I got stung by bees. I broke my toe trying to get away from them. Thirty five bee stings in one second, they said. I can't feel one side. But, it was my bad side, anyway."]*

NURSE. I'm sorry?

DOCTOR. It wath my bad thide. For dayging pithurth. *["It was*

42

my bad side. For taking pictures."'

NURSE. Thank goodness your good side was twice as good-looking to begin with. Maybe we'll take some pictures this afternoon.

DOCTOR. Thang you. You are nod thow bad yourthelve. Do wee haff thum way of reathing him? *["Thank you. You are not so bad yourself. Do we have some way of reaching him?"]*

NURSE. He'll let us know.

DOCTOR. *(To Man.)* You ghan alwaith contag uth, here. *(Pause.)* Whad a fath winder. Lod off yhangeh. *["You can always contact us here. What a fast winter. Lots of changes."]*

NURSE. I'm sorry, Doctor?

DOCTOR. Lahdz, ough, yhanghes. *["Lots, of, changes."]*

NURSE. *(She doesn't understand.)* Yes.

DOCTOR. Ihthh — *(He has to swallow.)* Ith your vhamly gumming? *["Is — Is your family coming?"]*

NURSE. We called a taxi. *(To Man.)* Which you should get out front for. And we have some new people arriving. May I walk you to your office?

DOCTOR. Thang you. All hride. Bhee goohd. Wheel mith you. *["Thank you. All right. Be good. We'll miss you."]*

MAN. Thank you, Doctor. Good-bye. I loved — I was — Thank you. *(In the following two lines, Prologue and Epilogue both begin to speak over one another, then Prologue needs to pause to drink some water.)*

PROLOGUE. Later, the Doctor is in his office, the Nurse —

EPILOGUE. Not that anyone cares, but — *(Epilogue stops, steps back, in a moment of kindness and deference, to allow Prologue to speak.)*

PROLOGUE. *(He clears his throat.)* Later, the Doctor is in his office, the Nurse in hers. The body of the woman, gone, and the tiny empty swaddling clothes on a shelf in a store, unbought. The body of the man is in a taxi, and then on a train. He sees the reflection of his reflection looking out the tinted window and sees the land and trees fly past. Towns fly by. People. "Whad a fath winder." There is a long long pause, no sound at all — it is like the quiet I deprived us of at the start of this. Excuse me. *(He exits.)*

EPILOGUE. It is neither not winter nor not summer. The body of the man, some man, is in another white room, alive, staring at another white wall. There was never any woman, never any nurse, nor doctor, nor certainly any man. Isn't that sad. There was never any abortion. There was no toy airplane. It was a pile of words. Isn't that sad.

PROLOGUE. *(Enters with flowers.)* The sun is setting, the great

43

sad past in the air, all of your life is in the air this evening. Another sunset, another dusk. The doctor and the nurse soldier on. The beauty of the suffering, suffering.

EPILOGUE. Life. Writing. Try again some other year. This was a mess. The wrong words at the wrong time. This is awful. So sorry. So cold.

NURSE. Isn't it a pretty light? Aren't we lucky.

DOCTOR. Yes. It's a very pretty light. We are lucky.

NURSE. Doesn't it look quiet.

PROLOGUE. Thank you for coming. The End. Good night.

EPILOGUE. Thank you for coming. There is no end. Good night.

DOCTOR. It does look quiet. *(Prologue has his bouquet of flowers, and, in a simple gesture, he turns, as if about to present them to someone, but, not knowing to whom he should give them, he lets them lower again by his side, as lights fade.)*

End of Play

PROPERTY LIST

Candle (lit)
Bowl of plastic fruit
Form (DOCTOR)
Watch (DOCTOR)
Notepad (DOCTOR, NURSE)
Pens (DOCTOR, NURSE)
Appointment book (DOCTOR)
Balsa wood toy airplane unassembled and one assembled (MAN)
Scarf (NURSE)
Dictionary (MAN)
Glass of water (PROLOGUE)
Bouquet of flowers (NURSE, PROLOGUE)
Sweater (NURSE)
Tray of food (DOCTOR)
Heart-shaped box of candy (PROLOGUE)
Telephone (DOCTOR)
Bag marked "Patient's Belongings" (MAN)
Bottle of pills (WOMAN)
Paperwork (NURSE)

NEW PLAYS

★ **THE GREAT AMERICAN TRAILER PARK MUSICAL music and lyrics by David Nehls, book by Betsy Kelso.** Pippi, a stripper on the run, has just moved into Armadillo Acres, wreaking havoc among the tenants of Florida's most exclusive trailer park. "Adultery, strippers, murderous ex-boyfriends, Costco and the Ice Capades. Undeniable fun." *–NY Post.* "Joyful and un-ashamedly vulgar." *–The New Yorker.* "Sparkles with treasure." *–New York Sun.* [2M, 5W] ISBN: 978-0-8222-2137-1

★ **MATCH by Stephen Belber.** When a young Seattle couple meet a promi-nent New York choreographer, they are led on a fraught journey that will change their lives forever. "Uproariously funny, deeply moving, enthralling theatre." *–NY Daily News.* "Prolific laughs and ear-to-ear smiles." *–NY Magazine.* [2M, 1W] ISBN: 978-0-8222-2020-6

★ **MR. MARMALADE by Noah Haidle.** Four-year-old Lucy's imaginary friend, Mr. Marmalade, doesn't have much time for her—not to mention he has a cocaine addiction and a penchant for pornography. "Alternately hilarious and heartbreaking." *–The New Yorker.* "A mature and accomplished play." *–LA Times.* "Scathingly observant comedy." *–Miami Herald.* [4M, 2W] ISBN: 978-0-8222-2142-5

★ **MOONLIGHT AND MAGNOLIAS by Ron Hutchinson.** Three men cloister themselves as they work tirelessly to reshape a screenplay that's just not working—*Gone with the Wind.* "Consumers of vintage Hollywood insider stories will eat up Hutchinson's diverting conjecture." *–Variety.* "A lot of fun." *–NY Post.* "A Hollywood dream-factory farce." *–Chicago Sun-Times.* [3M, 1W] ISBN: 978-0-8222-2084-8

★ **THE LEARNED LADIES OF PARK AVENUE by David Grimm, trans-lated and freely adapted from Molière's *Les Femmes Savantes*.** Dicky wants to marry Betty, but her mother's plan is for Betty to wed a most pompous man. "A brave, brainy and barmy revision." *–Hartford Courant.* "A rare but welcome bird in contemporary theatre." *–New Haven Register.* "Roll over Cole Porter." *–Boston Globe.* [5M, 5W] ISBN: 978-0-8222-2135-7

★ **REGRETS ONLY by Paul Rudnick.** A sparkling comedy of Manhattan manners that explores the latest topics in marriage, friendships and squandered riches. "One of the funniest quip-meisters on the planet." *–NY Times.* "Precious moments of hilarity. Devastatingly accurate political and social satire." *–BackStage.* "Great fun." *–CurtainUp.* [3M, 3W] ISBN: 978-0-8222-2223-1

DRAMATISTS PLAY SERVICE, INC.
440 Park Avenue South, New York, NY 10016 212-683-8960 Fax 212-213-1539
postmaster@dramatists.com www.dramatists.com